ALL YOU NEED IS A

THE RAINY DAY ACTIVITY BOOK

Games, Doodling, Puzzles, and More!

JOE RHATIGAN
ILLUSTRATIONS BY ANTHONY OWSLEY

imagine!

To Dad, who always seemed to know when I needed a new activity book.

An Imagine Book
Published by Charlesbridge
85 Main Street, Watertown, MA 02472
(617) 926-0329
www.charlesbridge.com

ISBN 978-1-62354-009-8
2 4 6 8 10 9 7 5 3 1

For information about custom editions, special sales, premium and corporate purchases,
please contact Charlesbridge Publishing at specialsales@charlesbridge.com

Dear Rain, Rain,

You know how I'm always telling you to go away, come again another day? Well, forget all that! From now on, feel free to stick around as long as you'd like. Make yourself at home. Stay awhile. Pour your heart out. Why? Because now I've got this really cool book packed with awesome things to do when you're out there wreaking havoc on picnics, baseball games, bike rides, swimming . . . you know, when going outside just isn't going to happen. This book's got puzzles, games, things to draw and doodle, fun activities with socks and pennies, quizzes, and lots more. I can take this book in the car when we go on long trips, I can take it with me when I have to go to Grandma's house (she's lovely, but her television only gets three channels), and when I take it to the dentist's office, I don't even hear the patients screaming! So, stick around as long as you'd like. You can even play if you want. Just don't get the pages wet, okay?

Yours truly,

_____

(sign your name here)

ALL ABOUT ME

Name:

_____

Age:

_____

Birthday:

_____

Hometown:

_____

Family members:

_____

Best friends:

_____

School:

_____

Grade:

_____

Favorite meal:

_____

Favorite song:

_____

When I was a little kid, I wanted to be a _____ when I grew up. Now I want to be a _____ when I grow up because ____
_____.

What is the best dream you've ever had?

_____

_____

_____

_____

What is the scariest nightmare you've ever had?

_____

_____

_____

_____

What would you do with one million dollars?

_____

_____

_____

_____

_____

You've been granted three wishes. What are they?

_____

_____

_____

_____

What superpower would you most like to have?

_____

_____

_____

_____

Where is the first place you'd take a space
alien visiting Earth for the first time?

_____

_____

_____

_____

Where would you most like to travel? Why?

_____

_____

_____

_____

What time period would you travel to in a time machine? Why?

_____

_____

_____

_____

_____

If you could have any wild animal in the world as a pet, which would you choose?

_____
_____
_____
_____

Who would you most want to have a meal with? Why?

_____
_____
_____
_____
_____

What's your favorite day of the week? Why?

_____
_____
_____
_____
_____

What is your least favorite? Why?

_____
_____
_____
_____
_____

WHAT WOULD . . .

Draw 'em as you see 'em!

. . . a rooster look like if it were a robot?

. . . a car look like if it were made out of JELL-O?

. . . a house look like if it didn't have any corners?

. . . a skyscraper look like if a cake artist designed it?

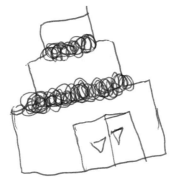

. . . a cow look like if it were an astronaut?

. . . a person look like if his nose, eyes, mouth, and ears were in the wrong spots?

. . . a hat look like if we had square heads?

. . . a hat look like if we had triangular heads?

. . . a polar bear look like in the tropics?

... a cat look like if it spent a lot of time at the gym?

... a pig look like with hair on its head and a beard?

... headphones look like if your ears were on your elbows?

SILLY SENTENCES

Fill in the blanks with the words from the list that sound like the words that best complete the sentences. The trick here is that each syllable of the words in the list acts as a full word itself in the answer. For example: He's very sick, but he won't <u>digest</u> yet. **Digest** sounds like **die just**: He's very sick, but he won't <u>die just</u> yet. **Answers on page 138.**

WORDS

~~amass~~
avenue
~~Canada~~
~~cattle~~
~~climate~~
counterfeit
dainty
~~ketchup~~
~~poker~~
wiggle

1. There's a mouse in the house, but don't worry. The _cattle_ get it.

2. Boy: How many legs does a spider have?
Girl: I don't know, I'll _____.

3. Daughter: The man from Denmark you invited over is thirsty.
Mom: Well, give the _____.

4. Mom's favorite way of waking up my sister is to _poker_.

5. Jerry's running behind. He'll _kethup_ with us later.

6. The tree is too tall, and I can't _climate_

7. Aunt Anita doesn't shake her head a lot because she's afraid her _____ fall off.

8. Our house was _amass_ after the cousins' visit.

9. Darling, can you reach up there and grab a _canada_ red beans?

10. They _____ math teacher because the old teacher retired.

MINI CROSSWORDS

These bite-size nugget crosswords are great for when you only have a few minutes (or if you have little patience!). The only thing is, you have to figure out which boxes the answers of the clues belong to. **Answers on page 138.**

AT DIFFERENT TEMPERATURES

Clue
Three forms of H2O

THREE-LETTER WORDS

Clues
Hot drink
What you do when you're hungry
Black sticky stuff
Tastes good with peanut butter
Rodent
To tear something
Glass container with a lid
A type of dance with metal-bottomed shoes

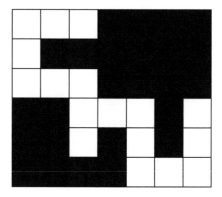

BAD FOR YOU ... BUT YUMMY

Clues
What's in your bag on Halloween
Bubbly sweet drink; also called *pop*.
They go well with milk
Fried thinly sliced potatoes
This has a hole in the middle
Sticky, stringy candy

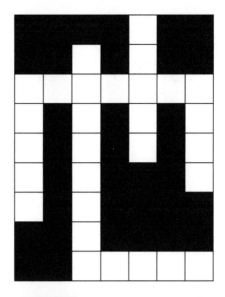

FIRST NAMES—MALE

Clues
Stanley, for short
Jonathan, for short
Theodore, for short
Joseph, for short
Harold, for short
Michael, for short
Richard, for short

FIRST NAMES—FEMALE

Clues
Katherine, for short
Margaret, for short
Elizabeth, for short (starts with a *B*)
Pamela, for short
Regina, for short
Samantha, for short
Susan, for short
Meghan, for short
Isabella, for short (starts with an *E*)

DIGITAL DELETIONS

This is a popular online game that's just as easy to play with paper and pencil. It's quick and fun, and after you play it a few times, you'll develop some strategies that will help you win!

The Object
Become the first person to erase all the numbers.

What You Need
2 players
Pencil

What You Do
1. Have one of the players write down a long number, using any number from zero to nine to compose it. For example: 839750150198395213. (The longer the number, the more fun the game!)
2. Each player takes a turn trying to erase the numbers until none are left. There are two ways to do this:
   a. Change any one of the digits to a value less than the number. For example, you can change a 7 to a 6, 5, 4, 3, 2, 1, or 0. So, the first player could change our number above to:
      839050150198395213.
   b. Erase a 0 and all the numbers to the right of it. For example, the second player could erase the 0 that the first player just created to make this number: 839.
3. The player who removes the last number wins. So, player one can do this: 835.
   Player 2: 805.
   Player 1: 8
   Player 2: 0
   Player 1: Erases the 0 and wins!

SQUIGGLE ART

Get someone to draw a squiggle below. Try to draw something using the squiggle—you could change it into an animal or a vehicle, or maybe a space alien. On the following page, draw a squiggle for a friend and let them create!

LOST YOUR MARBLES?

It may look like there are a lot of lost marbles to be found in the word search puzzle below, but actually, the word **MARBLES** can only be found once. Can you find it? **Answer on page 138.**

HAVE YOU SEEN ME
? ?
LI'L SHOOTER

```
M A R B E L E L M A B E A M M
A M R B M E S A R R B L R R A
R L S A A L E L S M A B B S R
S L E B R A M S A A L R E R S
L R L M L E S A L M B A L L L
B M B L A S A B L A A R A L B
L A A L E R A R B R A L S B L
A B M M A R B E L E R A S L A
M S R L E B R L M L A A L M M
A L B R S A L E E E M S E E A
S E L A A A R B S S M R M S S
B S R M R M A R B R E S R B B
A M S B L E S R S E R E L S A
M A R B E L S S L B R A M L M
A B M M A R B E L M R A S L A
```

DON'T THINK TWICE: THE CLICHÉ EDITION

Answer the questions below as quickly as possible without putting too much thought into them. Time yourself and see how many you get right. Don't write in the book if you want to play with friends. **Answers on page 139.**

Scoring: Divide the number of seconds it took you to take the quiz by the number of questions you got correct. The lower your score, the better. For example, if it took you twenty seconds to get nine questions correctly answered, your score would be 2.2. If it took you twenty-five seconds to get all ten questions right, your score would be 2.5. So, in this case, speed was better than accuracy!

Hint: If you don't know an answer, skip it! Remember, the object of this quiz is not only to get as many correct answers as possible, but also to do it in as little time as possible.

1–3: Awesome!
4–6: Smarty-pants
7 & up: Not bad!

Fill in the blanks:

1. Too many _____ spoil the broth.

2. He's a _____ for punishment.

3. It got _____ in the shuffle.

4. To make a long _____ short . . .

5. Money doesn't grow on _____.

6. He woke up on the _____ side of the bed.

7. Where there's _____, there's fire.

8. She's working her _____ to the bone.

9. He grew up on the wrong side of the _____.

10. A fool and his _____ are soon parted.

MORSE CODE

Used in the olden days to send messages on an electrical telegraph, Morse code is a fun way to send a message to a friend. Tap a pencil or use a flashlight to get your message across.

A ·−	J ·−−−	S ···	1 ·−−−−
B −···	K −·−	T −	2 ··−−−
C −·−·	L ·−··	U ··−	3 ···−−
D −··	M −−	V ···−	4 ····−
E ·	N −·	W ·−−	5 ·····
F ··−·	O −−−	X −··−	6 −····
G −−·	P ·−−·	Y −·−−	7 −−···
H ····	Q −−·−	Z −−··	8 −−−··
I ··	R ·−·		9 −−−−·
			0 −−−−−

DRAW IT BY NAMING IT

Provide the missing piece of each drawing with words. See example below!

DEAR _____,
(YOUR NAME HERE)

An advice column is an article in a newspaper, in a magazine, or on the Internet written by someone who is supposedly good at giving advice to people. This person receives letters or e-mails from readers who are suffering some sort of difficulty that they need help solving, and the advice columnist tries his or her best to give them ideas on what to do. How good are you at giving advice? Answer these letters (which are actually plots from books and movies) and find out!

Dear _____,

I'm being followed by a mysterious creature who insists I eat the green food he has on his plate. I keep trying to get away from him, but everywhere I turn, there he is. I don't want to eat green food, but I don't think he'll ever go away until I try it. What should I do???

—Picky Eater

_____
_____
_____
_____
_____

Dear _____,

When my father remarried, I had high hopes that my stepmother and two stepsisters would be the loving family I always wanted. Unfortunately, my father died unexpectedly, and that's when the trouble started. My stepsisters sneer at me and treat me like their personal servant. I am forced to do all the housework, and I have to wear rags and sleep on a cold floor. And my stepmother . . . well, let's just say I'm sure she loves her cat more than she loves me. How will I ever get out of this predicament?

—Desperately Seeking Fairy Godmother

_____

_____

_____

_____

_____

Dear _____,

I'm currently hiding four Saint Bernard puppies in the basement, and I know my father's going to flip if he finds them because we already have a dog and we don't have a lot of money right now! But I'm afraid the puppies' original owner might hurt them. I know my father is going to make me give them back. What should I do?

—Loves Big Dogs

_____

_____

_____

_____

_____

Dear _____,

I'm a toy who can actually move and talk when there are no humans around. My human is about to go off to college, and although he put all the other toys (my best friends) in the bag that goes in the attic, he put me in his suitcase. So even though I'm extremely happy that I get to stay with my human, I feel bad for my friends. What should I do?

—Confused Cowboy

_____

_____

_____

_____

_____

_____

Dear _____,

I have superpowers just like my parents, but they've always said I'm not allowed to use them, so I haven't. But now that they're in trouble, they're all like, "Use your powers, honey." I would love to explore my superpowers more, but after years of being told I couldn't, I feel like my parents are being hypocritical. Can you help me out here?

—Invisible and Walled In

_____

_____

_____

_____

_____

_____

Dear _____,

I'm falling in love with this beautiful woman, but I don't know what to do. I'm this big ogre of a guy, and this woman is a princess to behold. Not only that, but she's getting married to a man I know isn't right for her. She hasn't met him yet, but I have, and he's tyrannical and mean, and has a really big head and small body. Should I tell her how I really feel, or just keep it to myself?

—Green with Envy

_____

_____

_____

_____

_____

_____

Did You Know?

In England, advice columnists are known as agony aunts or agony uncles.

IT'S YOUR JOB: T-SHIRT DESIGNER

If you didn't do your job, we'd all be walking around
wearing plain, white T-shirts!

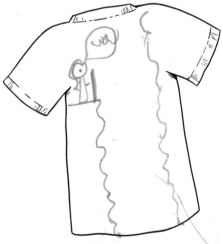

CONNECT 5

Mark five squares in a row to win this two-player game!

What You Do

1. Decide who will be X and who will be O.
2. The first player places his or her mark on any square on the board.
3. The second player places his or her mark on any square connected to the first player's square, either horizontally, vertically, or diagonally.
4. Players then alternate placing their marks on the board, always connected to one of the filled-in squares, until someone has five in a row.

Sample Game

Player one's first move

Player two's first move

Player one's second move

Umm . . . player two can't do that!

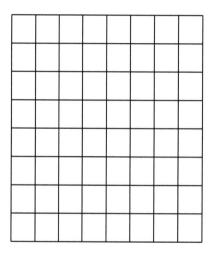

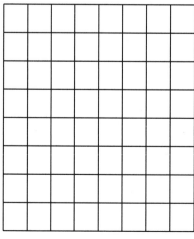

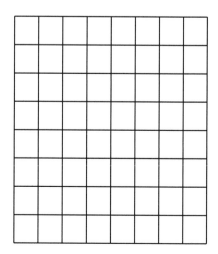

HINKY PINKY CROSSWORD

A hinky pinky is a riddle where the answer is two rhyming words. For example, a purple gorilla is a grape ape. All the answers to this crossword puzzle are hinky pinkys. **Answers on page 139.**

Across
2. Headgear for a feline
4. Hip ghost
6. Tinker Bell with a beard
8. Warm items for the feet of a red animal with a bushy tail
10. Flying grizzly
12. What you want from someone who agrees with you too much
14. Pickle named William
16. Icy fungus
17. Top worn by a female rodent

Down
1. Richard covered in syrup
2. Diamond gun
3. Rabbit comedian
5. Angry father
7. Goalkeeper for a game played with your feet
9. How a numbers class washes up
11. Huge hog
13. What you do on Michael's Facebook page
15. Not-very-nice ruler

IT'S YOUR JOB: COVER DESIGNER

Here are some interesting books. They need covers.

Don't Run with Art Supplies

Horror Weekend

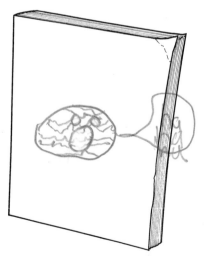

The Watermelon Gets His Revenge

The Mystery of the Missing Mailbox

Ghost School

Angry Mutant Squirrels Attack!

BAND NAME

One of the most difficult parts of starting a band is coming up with a cool name. Try these three tricks to see if you can find your dream band name. Then learn how to play an instrument or sing—you'll have a recording contract in no time!

1. Combine a word from list A with one from list B.

List A	List B
Brok'n	Cell Phone
Crackt	Clothesline
Dinosore	Desk Lamp
DJ	Gluv
Frankenstein	Melon
Heav-E	Mo
Miss Informed	Naptime
Nasty	Promises
OverLoded	Sock Drawer
Spiral	Toofpick

2. Find a dictionary, close your eyes, open to any page, and place your finger on the page. Add *The* to whatever word your finger is pointing to. You can repeat this a few times if you want a name with multiple words in it.

3. Smash two of your favorite words together. For example: Donkey + Edit = Donkit.

Now that you have your name, it's time to come up with a cool logo and design all the swag your fans can buy when they go to your concerts!

THE COLOR QUIZ

Match a color with the word or phrase to fill in the definitions. Colors can be used more than once and can be the first or last part of the word or phrase. Words and phrases are used only once. **Answers on page 139.**

1. _____: Unexpectedly
2. _____: An outcast
3. _____: A coward has this
4. _____: A medal for a wounded soldier
5. _____: Signifies a peaceful surrender
6. _____: What you get when you're fired
7. _____: Jealous
8. _____: First-place award
9. _____: To be happy
10. _____: Embarrassed
11. _____: A harmless untruth
12. _____: Bringing a homemade lunch to school or work
13. _____: Exceptional ability at gardening
14. _____: Specially priced restaurant meal
15. _____: Constant background noise
16. _____: Criticizing someone else for a quality you yourself possess
17. _____: Owing more money than you have
18. _____: The movies
19. _____: The brain
20. _____: Flowery, often romantic, writing

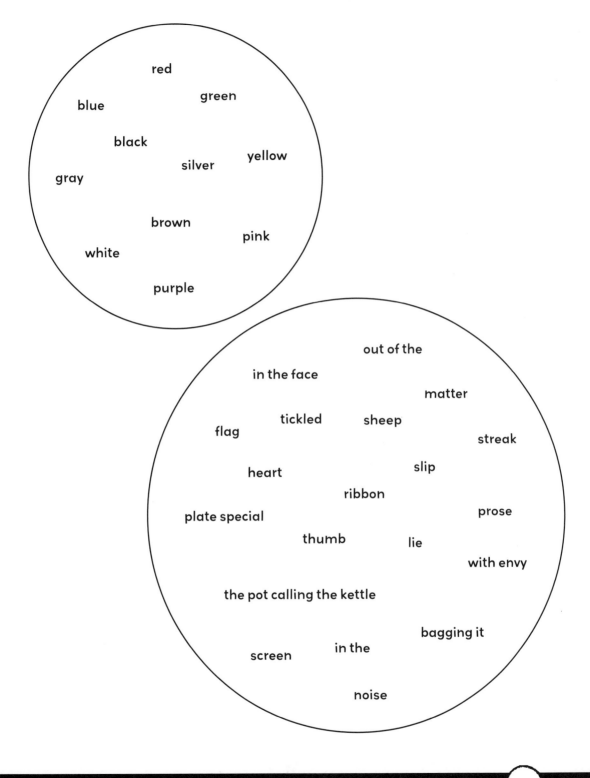

Circle 1 (top):

red

blue

green

black

yellow

silver

gray

brown

pink

white

purple

Circle 2 (bottom):

out of the

in the face

matter

tickled

sheep

flag

streak

heart

slip

ribbon

plate special

prose

thumb

lie

with envy

the pot calling the kettle

bagging it

screen

in the

noise

EYES SHUT GAMES

All these games have at least one thing in common: You have to close your eyes at some point to play them!

WHAT'S DIFFERENT?
This game challenges your powers of observation.

What You Need

2 players

What You Do

1. Have your partner look carefully at you, trying to memorize the details of your appearance.
2. Your partner then closes her eyes. You, meanwhile, have to change one thing about your appearance: If your collar was down, put it up; arrange your hair differently; unbutton a button; take off a bracelet.
3. When you're done, tell your partner to open her eyes. See if she can guess what changed.

Variation: You can also do this with rooms. Have the guesser leave the room, while the second player changes one thing about the room.

TIME FLIES
Do you (or any of your friends) know just how long a minute is?

What You Need

As many players as want to play
Watch with a second hand

What You Do

1. Choose a timekeeper, who will tell everyone when to close their eyes.
2. As the timekeeper keeps track of one full minute, everyone else tries to guess how long a minute is.
3. When a player thinks a minute has passed, she opens her eyes. The timekeeper marks the time each player's eyes opened. The player who guessed closest to one minute wins.

COIN TOSS

How good is your aim with your eyes closed?

What You Need

2 players
2 chairs
Large, plastic cup
Coin

What You Do

1. Place two chairs about three feet apart, facing each other. (You can move the chairs closer or farther away depending on your skill level.)
2. One player holds the cup, while the other has three turns to try to toss the coin in the cup. Oh, yeah—the person with the coin needs to close his eyes. The cup holder is not allowed to move the cup.
3. You get a point each time you get the coin into the cup. The first player to twenty points wins.

QUICK PICS

Can you draw while blindfolded? You're about to find out!

What You Need

3 players (if you only have 2, that's okay)
Drawing paper
Pencil or pen
Blindfold

What You Do

1. Choose who will be the originator, the artist, and the guesser. (Make sure you play at least three rounds so everyone gets a turn at each job.)
2. The originator writes down a word (an object or animal) on a scrap of paper and shows it to the artist. The guesser shouldn't see the word. (In the two-player version, the artist can just write down the word for himself.)
3. The artist then has to draw the object while blindfolded! The guesser attempts to figure out what the artist is drawing. Keep score if you wish, with each correct guess getting one point.

FUTOSHIKI

The object of Futoshiki is to place the numbers 1 to 4 (or higher, depending on the size of the puzzle) so that each row and column contains each of the digits. Some of the numbers are provided for you already. Also, greater than and less than signs must be obeyed: The number on the open side of a < or > symbol must be larger than the number on the pointed side. *Answers on page 139.*

Sample Game

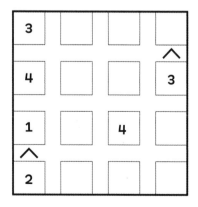

Step 1: It's always good to start by seeing if you can figure out any numbers based on the greater than and less than signs. In the first column, 2 is only greater than 1, so put the 1 in the box above the 2. This also lets you fill in the last blank box in that column: a 4.

Step 2: The third row is missing a 3 and a 2. Since there's already a 3 in the second row, fourth column, the 3 in the third row has to go in the second column. This means the 2 goes in the last box in the third row. Now you can fill in the rest of the fourth column, since 3 is greater than 1.

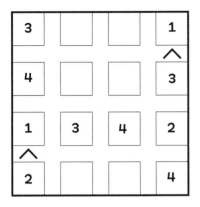

Step 3: The 4 in the first row can only go in the second square, since every other column already has a 4. Now you can fill in the box next to it with a 2. That 2 then shows that there's only one place left to place the 2 in the second row, and then the 1 in the same row.

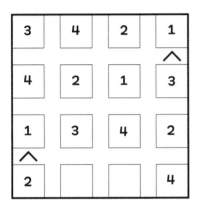

Step 4: The last two empty squares are now easy to fill in. The second column needs a 1 and the third column needs a 3.

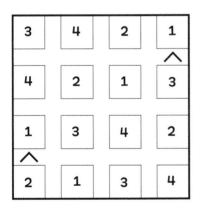

Tip: Often there will be two numbers or more that could fit in a certain box. Until you know for certain which number is the correct one, write both numbers in the box.

1.

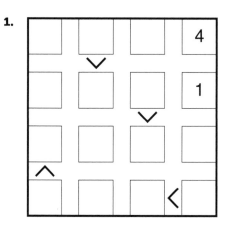

2.

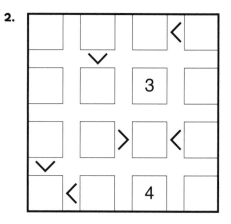

3.

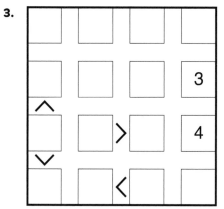

4.

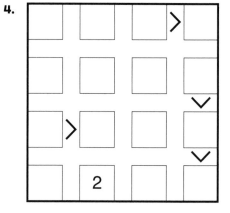

5.

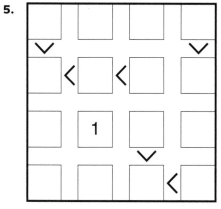

6.

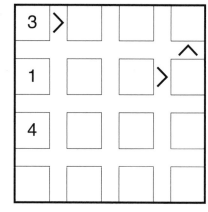

Now try a 5 x 5 puzzle, where you need to fill in the numbers 1 to 5.

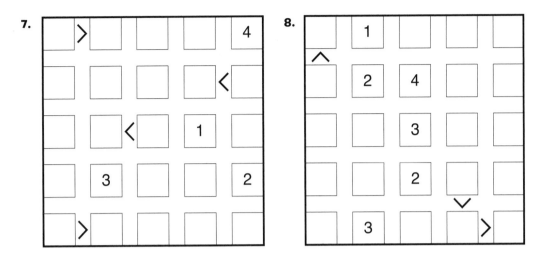

7.

8.

How about 6 x 6?

And finally, 7 x 7!

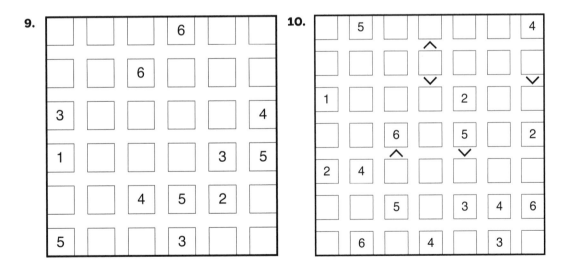

9.

10.

MONSTER MANIA

Here are some monster pieces. Draw the monsters that belong to them.

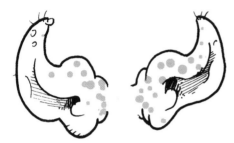

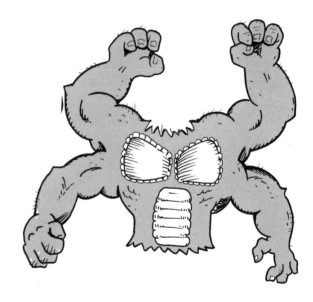

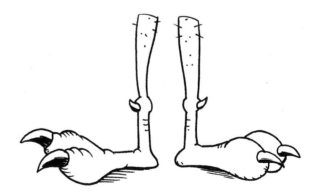

TWISTED TWISTERS

Time for a total mouth workout! Read these aloud with your friends for lots of laughs.

CLASSIC TWISTERS

Peter Piper picked a peck of pickled peppers.
A peck of pickled peppers Peter Piper picked.
If Peter Piper picked a peck of pickled peppers,
Where's the peck of pickled peppers Peter Piper picked?

You know New York,
You need New York,
You know you need unique New York.

How much wood would a woodchuck chuck
If a woodchuck could chuck wood?
He would chuck, he would, as much as he could,
And chuck as much wood as a woodchuck would
If a woodchuck could chuck wood.

Sally sells seashells by the seashore.
The shells Sally sells are surely from the sea.

A big black bug bit a big black bear,
then a big black bear bit the big black bug.
And when the big black bear bit the big black bug,
Then the big black bug bit the big black bear.

SHORT TWISTERS

Repeat each of these several times for the full effect!
Six thick thistle sticks.
Toy boat.
Red leather, yellow leather.
Stupid superstition!
World Wide Web.
Literally literary.
Greek grapes.

LONG TWISTERS

To sit in solemn silence in a dull, dark dock,
In a pestilential prison, with a lifelong lock,
Awaiting the sensation of a short, sharp shock,
From a cheap and chippy chopper on a big black block!
To sit in solemn silence in a dull, dark dock,
In a pestilential prison, with a lifelong lock,
Awaiting the sensation of a short, sharp shock,
From a cheap and chippy chopper on a big black block!
A dull, dark dock, a lifelong lock,
A short, sharp shock, a big black block!
To sit in solemn silence in a pestilential prison,
And awaiting the sensation
From a cheap and chippy chopper on a big black block!

—by W. S. Gilbert (of Gilbert and Sullivan), from *The Mikado*

Betty Botter had some butter,
"But," she said, "this butter's bitter.
If I bake this bitter butter,
it would make my batter bitter.
But a bit of better butter—
that would make my batter better."
So she bought a bit of butter,
better than her bitter butter,
and she baked it in her batter,
and the batter was not bitter.
So 'twas better Betty Botter
bought a bit of better butter.

A tree-toad loved a she-toad
Who lived up in a tree.
He was a two-toed tree-toad,
But a three-toed toad was she.
The two-toed tree-toad tried to win
The three-toed she-toad's heart,
For the two-toed tree-toad loved the ground
That the three-toed tree-toad trod.
But the two-toed tree-toad tried in vain;
He couldn't please her whim.
From her tree-toad bower,
With her three-toed power,
The she-toad vetoed him.

HEADACHE INDUCERS

I wish to wish the wish you wish to wish, but if you wish the wish the witch wishes, I won't wish the wish you wish to wish.

A skunk sat on a stump and thunk the stump stunk, but the stump thunk the skunk stunk.

Theophilus Thistler, the thistle sifter, in sifting a sieve of unsifted thistles, thrust three thousand thistles through the thick of his thumb.

Moses supposes his toeses are roses,
But Moses supposes erroneously,
For nobody's toeses are posies of roses
As Moses supposes his toeses to be.

Sure, Sally sold sixty shells at the sea's shore, but Sue sold seventy-seven! Sally, surprised at Sue's success, screamed and shouted seventeen times, "Sue's shells are shabby! Sally's shells are chic!" Sue said to Sally, "Say what?" Then Sue shouted, "Sally sold sixty-six shells, so she's upset. Sorry for shouting!"

Which wristwatches are Swiss wristwatches?

Many an anemone sees an enemy anemone.

BONUS

This isn't really a tongue twister, but memorizing and reciting this portion of the song "I Am the Very Model of a Modern Major-General" from Gilbert and Sullivan's *The Pirates of Penzance* will win you the admiration of many. Once you've got this down, find the full lyrics online and check out the many different performances of this song on YouTube.

I am the very pattern of a modern Major-General;
I've information vegetable, animal, and mineral;
I know the Kings of England, and I quote the fights historical,
From Marathon to Waterloo, in order categorical;
I'm very well acquainted, too, with matters mathematical,
I understand equations, both simple and quadratical,
About binomial theorem I'm teeming with a lot o' news,
With many cheerful facts about the square of the hypotenuse.
I'm very good at integral and differential calculus,
I know the scientific names of beings animalculous,
In short, in matters vegetable, animal, and mineral,
I am the very model of a modern Major-General.

MY PARENTS' PARTY

Find the numbers zero through twelve in this paragraph. For example, see where the number two is found in the following sentence: It won't happen again. **Answers on page 140.**

My gaze roams the room, taking in the amazing sight. On every table sits a breathtaking flower arrangement. But I can't find my little brother, and it worries me. Seth reeks of sweat and grass after playing in the yard, and he needs a bath before the celebration. A few friends had agreed to staff our parents' surprise wedding anniversary party, and they smile as they walk by me wearing black jackets and pants. Marty lets me try a cream puff. I've always loved appetizers! Yes, today is my parents' sixteenth anniversary, and even though I'm nervous, even though I can barely breathe and the weight of this day lies heavily on me, I plan on having some fun. I finally find Seth picking at the large pan of linguini.

Never again will I trust him to take care of himself! How I wish there was such a thing as little brother detention! Seth doesn't care how I feel, even though he can see how angry I am. I march him upstairs just as I hear the guests downstairs yell "Surprise!" I want to cry, but right then, my little brother shows me the card he wrote, which says, *Mom and Dat, We Lve U!*

These poor people are getting rained on! But what's it raining?
Cats and dogs, marshmallows and chocolate? You decide.

CAN YOU RAED TIHS?

In 2003, a viral e-mail hit the Internet, and it said this:

Aoccdrnig to rscheearch at Cmabrigde Uinervtisy, it deosn't mttaer in waht oredr the ltteers in a wrod are; the olny iprmoetnt tihng is taht the frist and lsat ltteer be at the rghit pclae. The rset can be a ttaol mses and you can sitll raed it wouthit a porbelm. Tihs is bcuseae the huamn mnid deos not raed ervey lteter by istlef, but the wrod as a wlohe. Amzanig, huh?

Did you have any trouble reading it? Well, according to the e-mail, you should be able to read it just fine! (If you can't, turn to page 141.) And while it turns out that it was not actually based on research done at Cambridge University (it's never a good idea to base all your scientific knowledge on chain e-mails!), it's still fun!

Here are some famous quotes that are also rearranged. See if you can figure out what they are. **Answers on page 141.**

1. All wrok and no paly mkaes Jcak a dlul boy.

2. Wehn the gnoig gtes tugoh, the tguoh get ginog.

3. It was a drak and smotry nhigt . . .

4. Bteetr to ramien seilnt and be toughht a fool tahn to sepak out and rvomee all dubot.—Ahaarbm Lloincn

5. Aoictn sepkas ledour tahn wrods, but not nraely as oeftn.—Mrak Tiawn

6. Eervy cilhd is an asitrt. The poblrem is to rmeian an asitrt ocne tehy gorw up.—Pbalo Psicsao

7. The rian in Saipn satys mnialy in the pilan.

8. And so, my folelw Anmeacris, ask not waht yuor ctuonry cna do fro yuo; aks waht yuo cna do fro yuor ctuonry.—Jhon F. Knneedy

9. The wsie man has lnog eras and a sorht tuogne.

10. I hvae fniedrs in oerllavs wsohe fishdeirnp I wulod not sawp for the fvaor of the knigs of the wlrod.—Tomhas Esoidn

Now cmoe up wtih yuor own to smutp yuor fdreins!

DOMINEERING

The object of this game is to be the last player able to make a successful move.

What You Need

2 players
Pencil or pen

What You Do

1. Decide who will be horizontal and who will be vertical. Also choose who will go first.

2. Using one of the game boards on the following pages, take turns connecting two dots. The horizontal player can only connect horizontally, and the vertical player can only connect vertically.

3. The first person unable to connect two dots loses.

IT'S ALL IN THE DETAILS

You can play this game by yourself or with friends. Each person should have a piece of paper (you can use the space below) and a pencil or some markers. Draw the scene described below, adding as much detail as possible in five minutes. Once time is up, turn the page and use the guide there to add up how many points you got for your details.

OUT ON THE WATER

You're on a boat out in the ocean. It's hot out. The captain says the wind should pick up shortly and you'll be home in time for dinner.

Scoring Guide

The artist drew himself: 5 points
The artist drew a life jacket on herself: 15 points
The boat has portholes on its side: 15 points
The boat has sails: 20 points
Each fish the artist drew in the water: 5 points
Each bird the artist drew in the air: 5 points
The artist drew sweat on himself: 5 points
The artist drew sweat on the captain: 10 points
The captain has a captain's hat: 10 points
The artist drew the sun: 10 points

Your score: _____

Player 2's score:
Player 3's score:
Player 4's score:

A WINTER SCENE

It's a cold and windy day, and you're standing in a snowy field. There's a lake nearby, and animals scurry this way and that, looking for food. Someone built a snowman near a tree stump.

Scoring Guide

The artist drew herself in the field: 10 points
The artist remembered to draw the lake: 5 points
The artist made it a frozen lake: 10 points
The artist drew ice skaters on the lake: 15 points
The artist somehow showed wind blowing: 20 points
Each different type of animal the artist drew: 5 points
The artist drew birds flying: 10 points
Each tree the artist drew: 5 points
The artist drew a hat for the snowman: 5 points
The snowman has arms: 10 points
The snowman has buttons on its "shirt": 10 points

Your score: _____

Player 2's score:
Player 3's score:
Player 4's score:

A DAY IN CLASS

You're in math class and the teacher is asking a question about long division.

Each student the artist drew: 5 points
The teacher is wearing glasses: 10 points
Each student whose hand is raised: 5 points
There's a blackboard in the classroom: 10 points
There's a math problem on the blackboard: 20 points
The teacher is holding something in her hands: 10 points
Every book the artist drew in the classroom: 5 points
The classroom has a door: 15 points
The teacher's shirt has buttons: 10 points
There's artwork on the classroom's walls: 20 points

Your score: _____

Player 2's score:
Player 3's score:
Player 4's score:

Now come up with your own scenario and scoring guide here, and test it out on your friends.

_____

_____

_____

_____

_____

_____

_____

_____

Scoring Guide

_____: _____ points

_____: _____ points

_____: _____ points

_____: _____ points

_____: _____ points

_____: _____ points

_____: _____ points

POEM HUNT

Writing poems can be a lot of fun, though lots of people think it's too difficult. Well, not anymore! On the next page is the text of Abraham Lincoln's Gettysburg Address, considered one of the best political speeches ever. Your job is to pick out words you like, cross out the rest, and then read the poem you created. For example:

~~Twinkle, twinkle,~~ little ~~star,~~
~~How I wonder what~~ you ~~are.~~
Up above the ~~world so high~~
~~Like a~~ diamond ~~in the~~ sky.
~~Twinkle,~~ twinkle, ~~little star,~~
~~How I wonder~~ what you are.

Okay, perhaps that doesn't make too much sense—but it's funny! And that's all that matters here.

Variation: Collect the words you like, cross out the rest, and rearrange the words below until a poem emerges! You can rearrange your words here if you want.

_____

_____

_____

_____

_____

_____

_____

Four score and seven years ago our fathers brought forth on this continent a new nation, conceived in liberty, and dedicated to the proposition that all men are created equal.

Now we are engaged in a great civil war, testing whether that nation, or any nation so conceived and so dedicated, can long endure. We are met on a great battlefield of that war. We have come to dedicate a portion of that field, as a final resting place for those who here gave their lives that that nation might live. It is altogether fitting and proper that we should do this.

But, in a larger sense, we can not dedicate—we can not consecrate—we can not hallow—this ground. The brave men, living and dead, who struggled here, have consecrated it, far above our poor power to add or detract. The world will little note, nor long remember what we say here, but it can never forget what they did here. It is for us, the living, rather, to be dedicated here to the unfinished work which they who fought here have thus far so nobly advanced. It is rather for us to be here dedicated to the great task remaining before us—that from these honored dead we take increased devotion to that cause for which they gave the last full measure of devotion—that we here highly resolve that these dead shall not have died in vain—that this nation, under God, shall have a new birth of freedom—and that government of the people, by the people, for the people, shall not perish from the earth.

Now try it with part of Chapter 26 of Bram Stoker's **Dracula.**

29 October.—This is written in the train from Varna to Galatz. Last night we all assembled a little before the time of sunset. Each of us had done his work as well as he could, so far as thought, and endeavour, and opportunity go, we are prepared for the whole of our journey, and for our work when we get to Galatz. When the usual time came round Mrs. Harker prepared herself for her hypnotic effort, and after a longer and more serious effort on the part of Van Helsing than has been usually necessary, she sank into the trance. Usually she speaks on a hint, but this time the Professor had to ask her questions, and to ask them pretty resolutely, before we could learn anything. At last her answer came.

"I can see nothing. We are still. There are no waves lapping, but only a steady swirl of water softly running against the hawser. I can hear men's voices calling, near and far, and the roll and creak of oars in the rowlocks. A gun is fired somewhere, the echo of it seems far away. There is tramping of feet overhead, and ropes and chains are dragged along. What is this? There is a gleam of light. I can feel the air blowing upon me."

Here she stopped. She had risen, as if impulsively, from where she lay on the sofa, and raised both her hands, palms upwards, as if lifting a weight. Van Helsing and I looked at each other with understanding. Quincey raised his eyebrows slightly and looked at her intently, whilst Harker's hand instinctively closed round the hilt of his Kukri. There was a long pause. We all knew that the time when she could speak was passing, but we felt that it was useless to say anything.

Suddenly she sat up, and as she opened her eyes said sweetly, "Would none of you like a cup of tea? You must all be so tired!"

We could only make her happy, and so acquiesced. She bustled off to get tea. When she had gone Van Helsing said, "You see, my friends. He is close to land. He has left his earth chest. But he has yet to get on shore. In the night he may lie hidden somewhere, but if he be not carried on shore, or if the ship do not touch it, he cannot achieve the land. In such case he can, if it be in the night, change his form and jump or fly on shore, then, unless he be carried he cannot escape. And if he be carried, then the customs men may discover what the box contain. Thus, in fine, if he escape not on shore tonight, or before dawn, there will be the whole day lost to him. We may then arrive in time. For if he escape not at night we shall come on him in daytime, boxed up and at our mercy. For he dare not be his true self, awake and visible, lest he be discovered."

There was no more to be said, so we waited in patience until the dawn, at which time we might learn more from Mrs. Harker.

Early this morning we listened, with breathless anxiety, for her response in her trance. The hypnotic stage was even longer in coming than before, and when it came the time remaining until full sunrise was so short that we began to despair. Van Helsing seemed to throw his whole soul into the effort. At last, in obedience to his will she made reply.

"All is dark. I hear lapping water, level with me, and some creaking as of wood on wood." She paused, and the red sun shot up. We must wait till tonight.

And so it is that we are traveling towards Galatz in an agony of expectation. We are due to arrive between two and three in the morning. But already, at Bucharest, we are three hours late, so we cannot possibly get in till well after sunup. Thus we shall have two more hypnotic messages from Mrs. Harker! Either or both may possibly throw more light on what is happening.

Later.—Sunset has come and gone. Fortunately it came at a time when there was no distraction. For had it occurred whilst we were at a station, we might not have secured the necessary calm and isolation. Mrs. Harker yielded to the hypnotic influence even less readily than this morning. I am in fear that her power of reading the Count's sensations may die away, just when we want it most. It seems to me that her imagination is beginning to work. Whilst she has been in the trance hitherto she has confined herself to the simplest of facts. If this goes on it may ultimately mislead us. If I thought that the Count's power over her would die away equally with her power of knowledge it would be a happy thought. But I am afraid that it may not be so.

When she did speak, her words were enigmatical: "Something is going out. I can feel it pass me like a cold wind. I can hear, far off, confused sounds, as of men talking in strange tongues, fierce falling water, and the howling of wolves." She stopped and a shudder ran through her, increasing in intensity for a few seconds, till at the end, she shook as though in a palsy. She said no more, even in answer to the Professor's imperative questioning. When she woke from the trance, she was cold, and exhausted, and languid, but her mind was all alert. She could not remember anything, but asked what she had said. When she was told, she pondered over it deeply for a long time and in silence.

Creatures from other worlds get hungry, too. Give them something **alien** to eat.

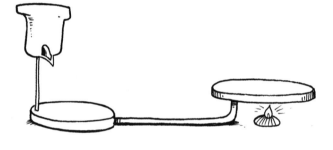

CHANGE ONE LETTER

Here's a game for people who like to play around with their words!

What You Need
1–4 players
Pencil or pen

What You Do
1. Choose someone to go first. This player picks a four-letter word and writes it down on the first line below.
2. The next player changes one letter of the word to create a new word.
3. The third player (or first again, depending on how many people are playing) then has to change one letter of the new word to create *another* word. This player cannot use the previous word.
4. Play continues until someone cannot come up with a new word.

For example:
Player one: stop
Player two: slop
Player one: slip
Player two: slim
Player one: slit
Player two: flit
Player one: flat
Player two: flap
And so on!

DON'T THINK TWICE: THE MONEY EDITION

Answer the questions below as quickly as possible without putting too much thought into them. Time yourself and see how many you get right. Don't write in the book if you want to play with friends. **Answers on page 141.**

Scoring: Divide the number of seconds it took you to take the quiz by the number of questions you got correct. The lower your score, the better. For example, if it took you twenty seconds to get nine questions correctly answered, your score would be 2.2. If it took you twenty-five seconds to get all ten questions right, your score would be 2.5. So, in this case, speed was better than accuracy!

Hint: If you don't know an answer, skip it! Remember, the object of this quiz is not only to get as many correct answers as possible, but also to do it in as little time as possible.

1–3: Awesome!
4–6: Smarty-pants
7 & up: Not bad!

Name who's on the money:

1. $1: _____

2. $0.25: _____

3. $50: _____

4. $0.10: _____

5. $5: _____

6. $0.05: _____

7. $10: _____

8. $100: _____

9. $0.01: _____

10. $20: _____

Bonus question
11. $1 gold coin: _____

OFF WITH ITS HEAD!

Cut off the first letter of what's being "beheaded" in each of the following questions to see what's left behind. For example: Behead eye water and leave behind a body part. Eye water = tear; beheaded tear = ear. **Answers on page 142.**

1. Behead a fluffy thing in the sky and leave a certain type of noise.

_____

2. Behead a snow particle and leave a body of water.

_____

3. Behead a pair of cubes used to play games and leave frozen water.

_____

4. Behead a storage cube and leave a large domestic animal.

_____

5. Behead a piece of furniture and leave what's on your head.

_____

6. Behead what's on your head and leave what you breathe.

_____

7. Behead a drinking vessel and leave a young girl.

_____

8. Behead a piece of sports equipment and leave everything.

_____

9. Behead a covering for your hands and leave what everybody wants.

_____

10. Behead another word for *slender* and leave what goes with a bow.

_____

11. Behead a pair of identical siblings and leave what you want to do at the end of a game.

_____

12. Behead a flying vehicle and leave a small road.

_____

13. Behead a distinctive odor and leave a penny.

_____

14. Behead a happy facial expression and leave 5,280 feet.

_____

15. Behead a shell-living creature and leave a fastening device that gets hammered in.

_____

16. Behead the device used to turn on your light and leave a magical woman.

_____

Now behead the first letter to get something that *sounds like* what remains, but is spelled differently. For example: Behead a small storage shelter (shed) and leave what's above your neck (hed = head).

17. Behead a woman and leave what you check for on your computer.

_____

18. Behead a direction giver and leave something you download onto your smartphone.

_____

19. Behead a belief or opinion and leave a large body of water.

_____

20. Behead what you watch on television and leave a garden instrument.

_____

Now come up with your own:

Behead _____ and leave _____.

Behead _____ and leave _____.

Behead _____ and leave _____.

Behead _____ and leave _____.

Behead _____ and leave _____.

Behead _____ and leave _____.

Behead _____ and leave _____.

Behead _____ and leave _____.

Behead _____ and leave _____.

Behead _____ and leave _____.

Behead _____ and leave _____.

Behead _____ and leave _____.

Behead _____ and leave _____.

Behead _____ and leave _____.

Behead _____ and leave _____.

Behead _____ and leave _____.

IT'S YOUR JOB: FORTUNE COOKIE WRITER

Some people think the best part of eating at a Chinese restaurant is getting the fortune cookie, breaking it open, and reading what your fortune will be. Ever wonder who writes the fortunes? Now you do!

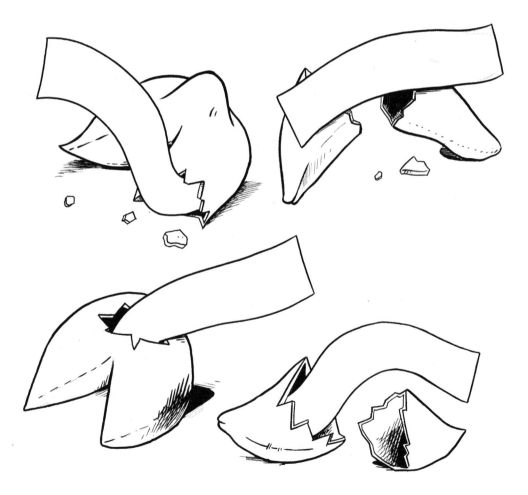

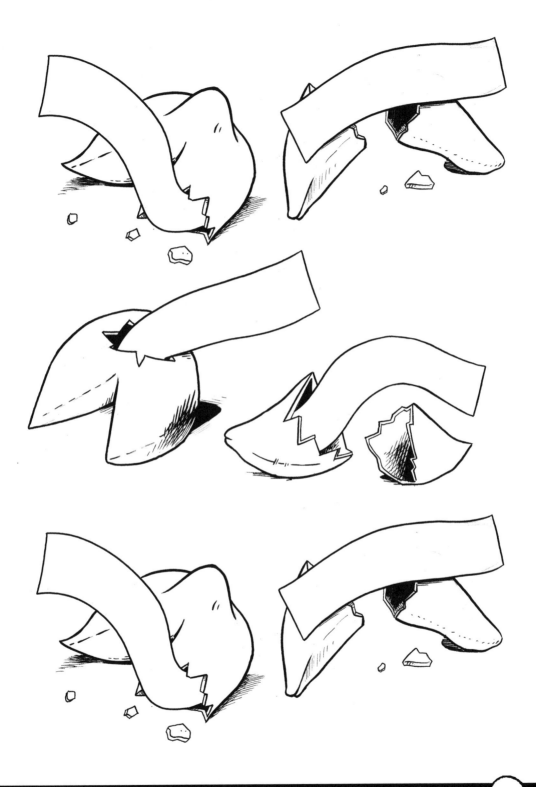

TEN TOTALLY USELESS THINGS TO DO

1. Memorize the alphabet . . . backward. It's one thing to know your ABCs, but can you learn your ZYXs? *Tip:* It's easier if you break them down into groups of three: ZYX WVU TSR QPO NML KJI HGF EDC BA.

2. Memorize how to count backward from 100 by 4s: 100, 96, 92, 88, 84, etc.

3. Try to move around your house without touching the floor. You can jump from chair to chair, use pillows or magazines as stepping stones, or get piggyback rides from an older sibling!

4. Count backward from 50 by 5, then add 3 so you're going backward, forward, backward, and so on: 50, 45, 48, 43, 46, etc.

5. Memorize the poem "Jabberwocky" by Lewis Carroll. Or just read it out loud with your friends!

'Twas brillig, and the slithy toves
Did gyre and gimble in the wabe;
All mimsy were the borogoves,
And the mome raths outgrabe.

"Beware the Jabberwock, my son!
The jaws that bite, the claws that catch!
Beware the Jubjub bird, and shun
The frumious Bandersnatch!"

He took his vorpal sword in hand:
Long time the manxome foe he sought—
So rested he by the Tumtum tree,
And stood a while in thought.

NO BANDERSNATCHES!

As in uffish thought he stood,
The Jabberwock, with eyes of flame,
Came whiffling through the tulgey wood,
And burbled as it came!

One, two! One, two! And through and through
The vorpal blade went snicker-snack!
He left it dead, and with its head
He went galumphing back.

"And hast thou slain the Jabberwock?
Come to my arms, my beamish boy!
O frabjous day! Callooh! Callay!"
He chortled in his joy.

'Twas brillig, and the slithy toves
Did gyre and gimble in the wabe;
All mimsy were the borogoves,
And the mome raths outgrabe.

6. Sit at a table with a bowl of cereal at the other end, out of reach. Try to use superhuman mind power to move the bowl toward you.

7. Create a rubber-band ball.

8. Build a fort out of pillows, couch cushions, blankets, and whatever else you can find. Don't let anyone else in unless they know the secret password, which is *Jabberwock* (see #5).

9. Have a philosophical conversation with a friend about which came first, the chicken or the egg.

10. Create a list of more useless things to do.

BULL'S "EYE"

The object of this game is to hit the eye on the bull's-eye.

What You Need

2 or more players
Penny for each player

What You Do

1. Tear out the image of the bull's face and lay it on a table or on the floor. Make sure each player has a penny.
2. Stand three to five feet back and take turns pitching your pennies onto the bull's eye.
3. Score each player according to the list below.
4. The highest score after ten rounds wins. Or play to an agreed-upon score, such as 101 points.
5. For an extra challenge, give players 50 points for landing on the pig below.

Scoring

Completely covering an eye and the coin is heads up: 10 points
Completely covering an eye and the coin is tails up: 15 points
Touching an eye and the coin is heads up: 5 points
Touching an eye and the coin is tails up: 7 points
Touching the face and the coin is heads up: 1 point
Touching the face and the coin is tails up: 3 points

Scoreboard

	Player 1	Player 2	Player 3	Player 4
Round 1				
Round 2				
Round 3				
Round 4				
Round 5				
Round 6				
Round 7				
Round 8				
Round 9				
Round 10				
Final Score				

WHAT JUST HAPPENED?

Something exciting, scary, unexpected, and/or hilarious is happening in each of the boxes below. We provided the noise; you provide the scene.

BANG!

POW!

KABOOOM!

POOF!

AAAAAAAAH!

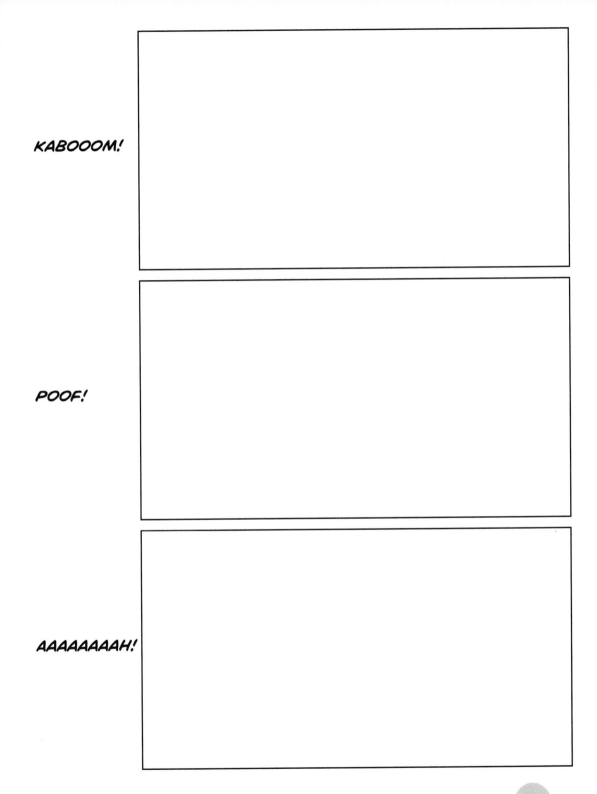

CLANK!

SWOOSH!

WHAM!

ZLOTT!

SPLOOSH!

VRONK!

PLAN YOUR MOST PERFECT DAY

You have been granted the most perfect twenty-four hours ever, where you can do whatever you want. Plan it on these pages. There's a catch, however: You have to do something different every hour and no repeats!

12 A.M.: _____

1 A.M.: _____

2 A.M.: _____

3 A.M.: _____

4 A.M.: _____

5 A.M.: _____

6 A.M.: _____

7 A.M.: _____

8 A.M.: _____

9 A.M.: _____

10 A.M.: _____

11 A.M.: _____

12 P.M.: _____

1 P.M.: _____

2 P.M.: _____

3 P.M.: _____

4 P.M.: _____

5 P.M.: _____

6 P.M.: _____

7 P.M.: _____

8 P.M.: _____

9 P.M.: _____

10 P.M.: _____

11 P.M.: _____

THE GREAT OUTLINE CHALLENGE

The simple drawings on this page look pretty obvious.
There's a bottle, a lamp, and more. Your challenge is to
draw **something else** in that space. Perhaps that guitar is
actually an old high-top sneaker or a dinosaur's head!

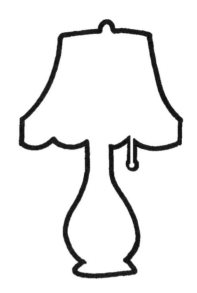

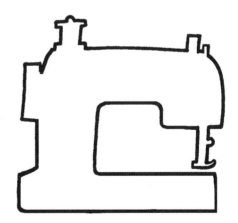

DON'T THINK TWICE: THE NICKNAME EDITION

Answer the questions below as quickly as possible without putting too much thought into them. Time yourself and see how many you get right. Don't write in the book if you want to play with friends. **Answers on page 142.**

Scoring: Divide the number of seconds it took you to take the quiz by the number of questions you got correct. The lower your score, the better. For example, if it took you twenty seconds to get nine questions correctly answered, your score would be 2.2. If it took you twenty-five seconds to get all ten questions right, your score would be 2.5. So, in this case, speed was better than accuracy!

Hint: If you don't know an answer, skip it! Remember, the object of this quiz is not only to get as many correct answers as possible, but also to do it in as little time as possible.

1–3: Awesome!
4–6: Smarty-pants
7 & up: Not bad!

List the proper names for the following nicknames:

1. Maggie: _Madie_

2. Jimmy: _Jim_

3. Chuck: _Chucky_

4. Dick: _____

5. Peggy: _Peay_

6. Bob: _Biby_

7. Bill: _Billy_

8. Beth: _Bethany_

9. Jack: _Jacky_

10. Xander: _Alexander_

Bonus question

11. Topher: _Topher_

TWO TRUTHS AND A LIE: HISTORY EDITION

Each of the following statements about history has two correct answers.
One is an outright lie. Can you find the fib? **Answers on page 142.**

1. George Washington . . .
A) never really chopped down a cherry tree.
B) never had any children of his own.
C) lived at the White House for only one of his two terms.

2. Sometimes leaders end up with unusual nicknames, including . . .
A) King Charles "the Simple" of France.
B) US President Bill "Slick Willie" Clinton.
C) King Barthos "the Bacteria-ridden" of Bavaria.

3. As crazy as it may sound . . .
A) not one, but *two* US presidents have reported seeing UFOs.
B) President Abraham Lincoln wrote in his diaries about an encounter with what he thought was a vampire.
C) President Teddy Roosevelt wrote about an encounter an associate of his had with Bigfoot.

4. World leaders have some interesting hobbies, including . . .
A) North Korea's Kim Jong Il, who loved movies so much he had a South Korean movie director and his movie star wife kidnapped so they could make movies for him.
B) Queen Elizabeth of England, who collects spoons that she steals from important dinners she attends.
C) King Charles of England (during the 1600s), who collected mummies of dead Egyptian pharaohs. (He liked to cover himself with mummy dust, hoping it would make him as great as the pharaohs.)

5. Ghosts have been known to inhabit the White House, including . . .
A) pop singer Michael Jackson, whose ghost is looking for a bathroom.
B) Abraham Lincoln, who haunts the Lincoln Bedroom.
C) First Lady Abigail Adams, whose ghost haunts the East Room, hanging laundry.

6. Some leaders have elaborate names and titles, including . . .
A) Lord Bathespane, an early king of England, who added this to his title: Protector of the Innocent, Punisher of the Wicked, Sword Master Second to None.
B) Idi Amin, the military dictator and president of Uganda from 1971 to 1979, who preferred this title: His Excellency, President for Life, Field Marshal Al Hadji Doctor Idi Amin Dada, VC, DSO, MC, Lord of All the Beasts of the Earth and

Fishes of the Seas and Conqueror of the British Empire in Africa in General and Uganda in Particular.

C) Pedro I, leader of Brazil during the early 1800s, whose full name was Pedro de Alcântara Francisco António João Carlos Xavier de Paula Miguel Rafael Joaquim José Gonzaga Pascoal Cipriano Serafim de Braganza e Bourbon.

7. US presidents are known for their curious tastes in pets, including . . .

A) James Madison and Woodrow Wilson, who both kept flocks of sheep on the White House lawn.

B) John Quincy Adams and Herbert Hoover, who both kept pet alligators.

C) George W. Bush and Barack Obama, who both let their daughters care for the twenty-foot python that was found on the White House grounds by a Secret Service agent.

8. Sports have been popular throughout history, including these interesting games:

A) ullamaliztli, a game played by the ancient Aztecs that was a little bit like soccer, except that the losing team's captain had his heart eaten by the fans.

B) wallaoomph, a game played during the Middle Ages in which armies used cows for catapult target practice. The cow closest to the person in the field won.

C) pankration, the ancient Greek game of no-rules wrestling (although it was considered bad form to actually kill your opponent).

9. Fashion has been around as long as we've been wearing clothes. Some fashion statements throughout history haven't always been wise choices, including . . .

A) hats with lightning rods attached to them. This became a fad during the 1770s in France after Benjamin Franklin invented the lightning rod.

B) dangerously tall high heels. Louis XIV of France (early 1700s) put Lady Gaga to shame when he began wearing high heels so he could appear taller (he was a short man). Soon his whole court was wearing heels—some as tall as six inches.

C) fire ties. When King Edward of England reached to grab a biscuit, putting his tie over a candle, men began emulating the event with ties that would slowly burn toward their neck. Things got ugly when the men fell asleep without putting the fire ties out first.

10. History books are full of stories of things that never happened. Which of these three statements is not true?

A) The public was never welcome at the White House except for guided tours.

B) Betsy Ross did not design the first American flag.

C) Christopher Columbus never set foot on the North American mainland.

CLOTHING MAKES THE CARTOON

Years ago, a false story circulated that said Finland had banned the cartoon character Donald Duck because he didn't wear any pants. This story gets you thinking ... Why do some cartoon characters wear clothes while others wear only pants, just a shirt, or nothing at all?

Using the chart below, place all the cartoon characters you know in the proper category and see if you can come up with any conclusions about this serious issue. After you're done with this, ponder this question: Why do cartoon characters always wear the *same* clothes?

Shirt and Pants	Shirt Only	Pants Only	Just About Naked	Fully Clothed

Now give these cartoon critters some clothes!

CLASSIC RIDDLES & CONUNDRUMS

Read these aloud to whomever's hanging around. If someone's heard one before, make sure he holds his tongue until everyone gets a chance to figure it out! **Answers on page 143.**

1. What can run but never walks, has a mouth but never talks, has a head but never weeps, and has a bed but never sleeps?

2. What is light as a feather, but even the strongest man cannot hold it more than a few minutes?

3. In a marble hall white as milk
Lined with skin as soft as silk
Within a fountain crystal-clear
A golden apple doth appear.
No doors there are to this stronghold,
Yet thieves break in to steal its gold.
What am I?

4. What is black when you buy it, red when you use it, and gray when you throw it away?

5. What walks on four legs in the morning, two legs in the afternoon, and three legs in the evening?

6. What did Adam and Eve give to their children that they never had themselves?

7. What is the one question you can never answer "yes" to?

8. My life can be measured in hours; I serve by being devoured. Thin, I am quick; fat, I am slow. Wind is my foe. What am I?

9. What goes up a chimney down, but won't go down a chimney up?

10. What's the only thing you'll break by saying its name?

11. What has two heads, four ears, six feet, and one tail?

12. I'm where yesterday follows today, and tomorrow's in the middle. What am I?

13. Pronounced as one letter, and written with three, two letters there are, and two only, in me. I'm double, I'm single, I'm black, blue, and gray, I'm read from both ends, and the same either way. What am I?

14. I never was, am always to be. No one ever saw me, nor ever will, and yet I am the confidence of all who live and breathe on this terrestrial ball. What am I?

15. The man who invented it doesn't want it. The man who bought it doesn't need it. The man who needs it doesn't know it. What is it?

16. You throw away the outside and cook the inside. Then you eat the outside and throw away the inside. What is it?

17. I am weightless, but you can see me. Put me in a bucket and I'll make it lighter. What am I?

18. Throw me off the highest building, and I'll not break. But put me in the ocean, and I will. What am I?

19. What was given to you, belongs to you, and yet is used more by your family and friends than by yourself?

20. What gets wetter and wetter the more it dries?

Bonus
As a whole, I am both safe and secure. Behead me, and I become a place of eating. Behead me again, and I am the partner of ready. Restore me, and I become the domain of beasts. What am I?

IT'S YOUR JOB: MONEY MAKER

The government wants you to design new money—and they want it to be wacky! Get to work on the bills and coins below. Don't forget to include the amount they are each worth!

PONDERABLES

There may be perfectly good answers to the following questions; however, we don't care about that. We want to know what *you* think. In the spaces provided, come up with your own logical (or illogical) conclusions.

1. There are A batteries, C batteries, and D batteries. What happened to B batteries?

_____

_____

2. Why do we park in a driveway and drive on a parkway?

_____

_____

3. What do fish do when they get thirsty?

_____

_____

4. Why is the word *abbreviation* such a long word?

_____

_____

5. How do you throw away a garbage can?

_____

_____

6. Sandwich meat is round. Bread is square. Explain.

_____

_____

7. If ghosts walk through walls, why don't they fall through floors?

_____

_____

8. Why do crackers have holes in them?

_____

_____

9. Why do you chop *down* a tree and then chop it *up*?

_____

_____

10. If vegetarians eat vegetables, what do humanitarians eat?

_____

_____

11. If corn oil comes from corn, where does baby oil come from?

_____

_____

12. Did early settlers go camping?

_____

_____

13. What happens if you get scared half to death . . . twice?

_____

_____

14. We know there's a speed of light, but what is the speed of dark?

_____

_____

15. What do you do if you see an endangered animal eating an endangered plant?

_____

_____

16. How do Styrofoam makers ship it?

_____

_____

WORD JUMBLES

Unscramble the words in each puzzle, and then use the shaded letters to form a word that fits in the sentence. Use the empty space on the pages to figure out the words. One trick is to place all the letters of a scrambled word in a circle. For example, the letters YPHPA may be difficult to sort out, but when placed like this:

```
        P
    P       H
      A   Y
```

it's easier to see the word is **happy**.

Answers on page 143.

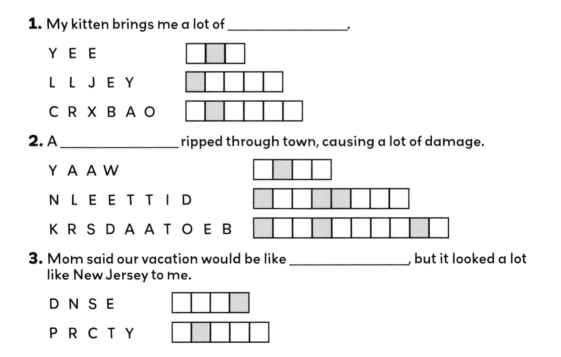

1. My kitten brings me a lot of _____.

Y E E

L L J E Y

C R X B A O

2. A _____ ripped through town, causing a lot of damage.

Y A A W

N L E E T T I D

K R S D A A T O E B

3. Mom said our vacation would be like _____, but it looked a lot like New Jersey to me.

D N S E

P R C T Y

C N E I P L   ☐☐☐☐☐☐

S S S I T T N A A   ☐☐☐☐☐☐☐☐☐

4. Word jumbles give me _____.

S E S C H   ☐☐☐☐☐

T R W R I E   ☐☐☐☐☐☐

V D R K R A A A   ☐☐☐☐☐☐☐☐

T H U O R D G   ☐☐☐☐☐☐☐

M I U E H L   ☐☐☐☐☐☐

5. Timmy wants a _____ for his birthday, but his mom says he's too young.

T S G E D I   ☐☐☐☐☐☐

S R I I P T   ☐☐☐☐☐☐

O S N A M R   ☐☐☐☐☐☐

T U T C E E L   ☐☐☐☐☐☐

HOW MANY . . .

Count 'em up!
Answers on page 143.

. . . rectangles and squares?
Hint: It's more than 10.

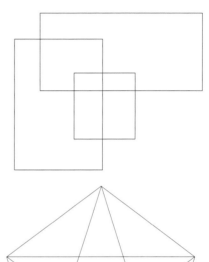

. . . triangles?
Hint: It's more than 10.

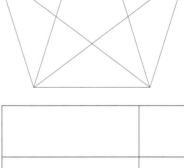

. . . rectangles and squares?
(This one is more difficult!)
Hint: It's more than 10.

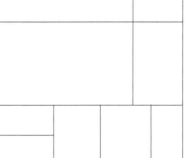

WORDS WITHIN WORDS

For each word listed below, add one letter to create a new word. Then add another letter to create yet another new word. Keep adding letters to create new words until you can't anymore. For example:

In
Sin
Sing
Sting
Siting
Sitting
Spitting

And so on!

to

_____
_____
_____
_____
_____
_____

am

_____
_____
_____
_____
_____

art

_____
_____
_____
_____
_____

in

_____
_____
_____
_____
_____
_____

an

_____
_____
_____
_____
_____

it

_____
_____
_____
_____
_____

me

la

all

no

at

we

do

ma

is

pa

BACK TO THE DRAWING BOARD

Just about everyone knows what the following famous cartoon and puppet characters look like. See if you can forget what your mind tells you they look like and reimagine them . . . from scratch.

SpongeBob SquarePants

Miss Piggy

Spider-Man

Dora the Explorer

Cookie Monster

Mickey Mouse

Arthur (the aardvark)

Winnie the Pooh

Daffy Duck

Bart Simpson

BATTLESHIPS

The object of this game is to guess the location of all your opponent's ships on the grid. It's just like the board game. Not so much like the movie.

What You Need
2 players
Pencil or pen for each player

What You Do

1. Tear out the grids on the following pages to play. Each player needs two grids: one to place his ships, and the other to note hits and misses. (When you run out of grids, create your own with graph paper.)

2. Without the other player seeing what you're doing, place your ships on one of the grids by shading in squares. These are the ships at your command:

> 1 aircraft carrier (5 squares)
> 1 battleship (4 squares)
> 1 cruiser (3 squares)
> 2 destroyers (2 squares)
> 2 submarines (1 square)

	1	2	3	4	5	6	7	8	9	10
A										▓
B		▓	▓	▓	▓					
C									▓	
D									▓	
E		▓	▓	▓					▓	
F									▓	
G		▓				▓				
H		▓				▓				
I										
J					▓					

3. Once each player has positioned his ships, take turns guessing where your opponent has hidden his ships by saying the letter and number of a particular square, such as E8.

4. The opponent says "miss" if you didn't hit a ship (pick a square that is shaded in) and says "hit" if you did.

5. Mark the hit or miss on the second grid to keep track of your opponent's ships.

6. The first player to have all his ships sunk loses.

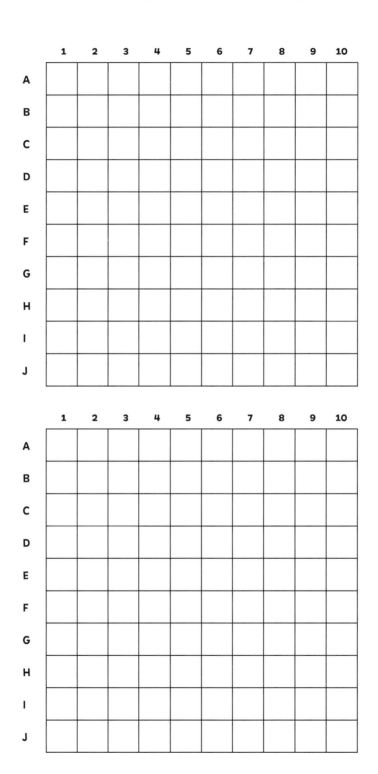

	1	2	3	4	5	6	7	8	9	10
A										
B										
C										
D										
E										
F										
G										
H										
I										
J										

	1	2	3	4	5	6	7	8	9	10
A										
B										
C										
D										
E										
F										
G										
H										
I										
J										

For this game you have to create as many words as possible inside your grid.

What You Need
2 or more players
Pencil or pen for each player

What You Do
1. Each player needs a 4 x 4 grid. You can tear out the grids on the following page or make your own.
2. Take turns naming a letter of the alphabet. You can use the same letter more than once.
3. As each letter is called out, each player must place it inside her grid.
4. When the grids are full, each player counts the number of words she was able to create vertically, horizontally, and diagonally.
5. The person with the most words wins.

Hint: You can choose letters that help you complete words, or you can stop your opponents from getting words by calling out *Z*, *X*, and other uncommon letters.

Sample Game

p	o	d	s
f	l	a	t
i	d	a	a
c	i	b	y

How many words do you see here? *Pod, pods, flat, at, old, stay, play*... We count at least twelve!

Variations: Only count the four-letter words, or count words written both forward and backward.

IT'S YOUR JOB: INTERIOR DESIGNER

Look at these barren rooms! Decorate! Decorate! Decorate!

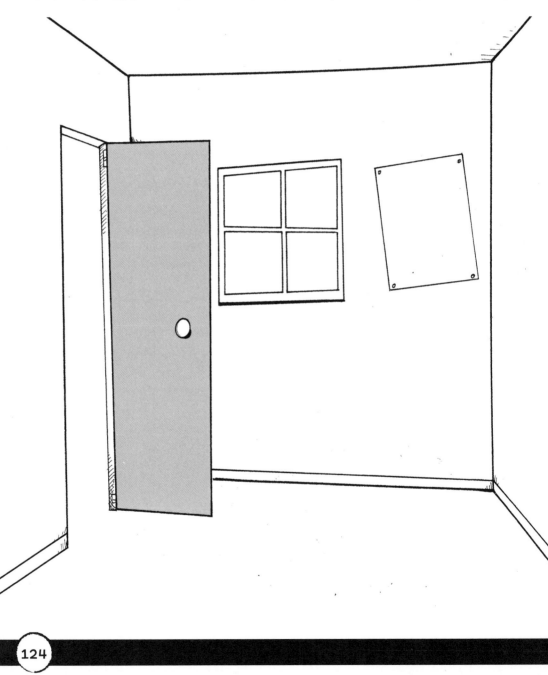

LADDER RACES

The object of this game is to create the shortest ladder between two words.

What You Need

2 players
Pencil or pen for each player

What You Do

1. You and your opponent each choose a word with the same number of letters. Player one's word is the starting word, and player two's word is the ending word.

2. You both now try to find a ladder between the words. A ladder is a sequence of words linked either by changing one letter to make another word or scrambling the order of the letters to make another word.

3. The player with the shortest ladder wins. If neither can find a ladder, it's a tie.

Sample Game

Player one chooses the word *sock* and player two chooses the word *call*.

Sock
Sack (changed one letter to make another word)
Lack (changed one letter to make another word)
Calk (scrambled order of letters to make another word)
Call (changed one letter to make another word)

SOCK
Sack
Lack
Calk
CALL

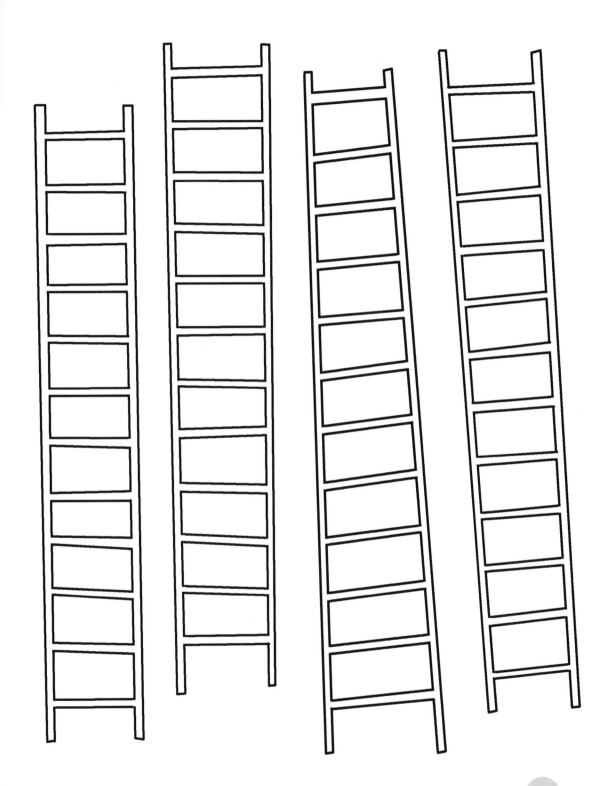

STACK 'EM HIGH

How high can you stack the dishes, books, blocks, fruit, cups, and hamsters before they fall over?

DO AS I SAY, NOT AS I DO

Getting mixed messages is confusing, isn't it?!

What You Need
4 or more players

What You Do
1. Select one player to be the leader.
2. The leader now tells the players what to do, while she acts out exactly the opposite. The other players must follow the leader's verbal direction, not what she is doing. (Be warned: This is harder than it sounds.) For example:
   Say, "Hands in your lap!" while flinging both hands up over your head.
   Say, "Scratch your chin!" while rubbing your nose.
   Say, "Rub your belly!" while tapping your chest.
3. If a player mimics the action instead of following the words, he's out! If the leader makes a mistake and acts out what she's saying instead of doing something different, she's out and it's the next player's turn to be the leader.
4. Keep going around the group until everyone gets a chance to be the leader.

Variations: Try alternating between doing what the leader says and doing what she does. Speed up! Have the leader do two different things with her right hand (tugging an earlobe) and left hand (rubbing an eyebrow), while giving different verbal directions ("Blink your eyes"). The players mimic both hand movements, or they mimic only one hand's movement.

NUMBER HUNT

Here's a scavenger hunt that takes some thinking.

What You Need
2 or more players
Some planning time

What You Do
1. Select someone to be the hunt master. This person goes around the home picking out items for the hunt. But this isn't a normal scavenger hunt! The hunt master finds groups of things and then puts them in a mathematical formula and hands out a copy to each player. For example:

> Number of windows on the second floor + number of cars in the driveway - houseplants x CDs in the living room (etc. The more items, the better!) = _____

2. Once all the items are found, all the players have to do is the math.

3. The first person to arrive at the starting point with the correct answer wins.

INDOOR VOLLEYBALL

Whatever you do, don't "spike" the ball!

What You Need
2 or more players
String
Blown-up balloon

What You Do
1. Tie the string across the living room or other open space, about one foot off the ground. Make sure to tie the string to something that won't fall over.
2. Divide your players into teams and have them set up on either side of the string in a crab-walk position (see illustration). No shoes!
3. Choose a team to serve first. That team throws the balloon up in the air and kicks it over the string.
4. The teams take turns kicking the balloon over the string until it falls on their own side. The other team gets a point whenever the other team lets the ball drop on the floor.
5. The first team to 21 points wins.

QUICK GAMES

BACKWARD DAY
Put your clothes on backward and see how your day goes.

JUGGLE SCARVES
Find three scarves and practice keeping them all up in the air. Works with tissues, too.

INVISIBLE TAG
Turn off the lights and play tag. The person who's It is the only one who can move. Everyone else must hide and remain perfectly still.

SOCK WRESTLING
Two players take off their shoes and one sock, leaving one sock on. They get on the ground in a large, mostly empty room and try to take off each other's sock. It's best to have an adult referee for this game!

SPARE PARTS

What can you draw using only the spare parts found below?

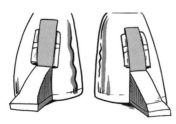

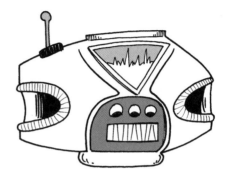

Silly Sentences (page 12)

1. cattle; 2. counterfeit; 3. dainty; 4. poker; 5. ketchup; 6. climate;
7. wiggle; 8. amass; 9. Canada; 10. avenue

Mini Crosswords (page 14)

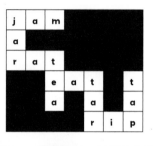
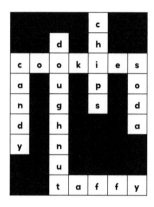
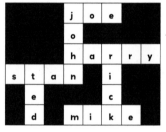

Lost Your Marbles? (page 20)

```
M A R B E L E L M A B E A M M
A M R B M E S A R R B L R R A
R L S A A L E L S M A B B S R
S L E B R A M S A A L R E R S
L R L M L E S A L M B A L L L
B M B L A S A B L A A R A L B
L A A L E R A R B R A L S B L
A B M M A R B E L E R A S L A
M S R L E B R L M L A A L M M
A L B R S A L E E E M S E E A
S E L A A A R B S S M R M S S
B S R M R M A R B R E S R B B
A M S B L E S R S E R E L S A
M A R B E L S S L B R A M L M
A B M M A R B E L M R A S L A
```

Don't Think Twice: The Cliché Edition (page 21)

1. cooks (or chefs); 2. glutton; 3. lost; 4. story; 5. trees; 6. wrong;
7. smoke; 8. fingers; 9. tracks; 10. money

Hinky Pinky Crossword (page 35)

Across

2. cat hat; 4. cool ghoul; 6. hairy fairy; 8. fox socks; 10. air bear; 12. less
yes; 14. dill Will; 16. cold mold; 17. mouse blouse

Down

1. sticky Ricky; 2. crystal pistol; 3. funny bunny; 5. mad dad; 7. soccer
blocker; 9. math bath; 11. big pig; 13. like Mike; 15. mean queen

The Color Quiz (page 40)

1. out of the blue; 2. black sheep; 3. yellow streak; 4. Purple Heart;
5. white flag; 6. pink slip; 7. green with envy; 8. blue ribbon; 9. tickled
pink; 10. red in the face; 11. white lie; 12. brown bagging it; 13. green
thumb; 14. blue plate special; 15. white noise; 16. pot calling the kettle
black; 17. in the red; 18. silver screen; 19. gray matter; 20. purple prose

Futoshiki (page 44)

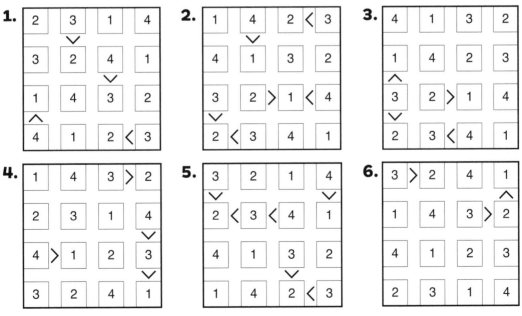

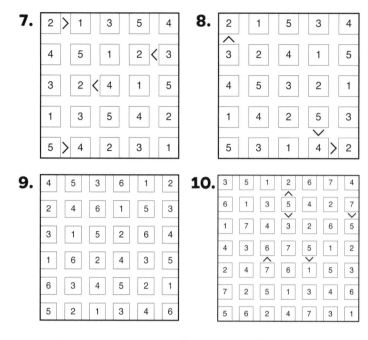

My Parents' Party (page 55)

My ga**ZE RO**ams the room, taking in the amazing sight. **ON E**very table sits a breathtaking flower arrangement. But I can't find my little brother, and i**T WO**rries me. Se**TH REE**ks of sweat and grass after playing in the yard, and he needs a bath before the celebration. A few friends had agreed to staf**F OUR** parents' surprise wedding anniversary party, and they smile as they walk by me wearing black jackets and pants. Marty lets me try a cream puf**F. I'VE** always loved appetizers! Yes, today is my parents' **SIX**teenth anniversary, and even though I'm nervou**S, EVEN** though I can barely breathe and the w**EIGHT** of this day lies heavily on me, I plan on having some fun. I finally find Seth picking at the large pan of lingui**NI. NE**ver again will I trust him to take care of himself! How I wish there was such a thing as little brother de**TEN**tion! Seth doesn't care how I fe**EL, EVEN** though he can see how angry I am. I march him upstairs just as I hear the guests downstairs yell "Surprise!" I want to cry, but right then, my little brother shows me the card he wrote, which says, *Mom and Da**T, WE LVE** U!*

Can You Raed Tihs? (page 58)

According to research at Cambridge University, it doesn't matter in what order the letters in a word are; the only important thing is that the first and last letter be at the right place. The rest can be a total mess and you can still read it without a problem. This is because the human mind does not read every letter by itself, but the word as a whole. Amazing, huh?

1. All work and no play makes Jack a dull boy.
2. When the going gets tough, the tough get going.
3. It was a dark and stormy night . . .
4. Better to remain silent and be thought a fool than to speak out and remove all doubt.—Abraham Lincoln
5. Action speaks louder than words, but not nearly as often.—Mark Twain
6. Every child is an artist. The problem is to remain an artist once they grow up.—Pablo Picasso
7. The rain in Spain stays mainly in the plain.
8. And so, my fellow Americans, ask not what your country can do for you; ask what you can do for your country.—John F. Kennedy
9. The wise man has long ears and a short tongue.
10. I have friends in overalls whose friendship I would not swap for the favor of the kings of the world.—Thomas Edison

Don't Think Twice: The Money Edition (page 78)

1. George Washington; 2. George Washington; 3. Ulysses S. Grant; 4. Franklin D. Roosevelt; 5. Abraham Lincoln; 6. Thomas Jefferson; 7. Alexander Hamilton; 8. Benjamin Franklin; 9. Abraham Lincoln; 10. Andrew Jackson; 11. Sacagawea

Off with Its Head! (page 79)
1. cloud = loud; 2. flake = lake; 3. dice = ice; 4. box = ox; 5. chair = hair;
6. hair = air; 7. glass = lass; 8. ball = all; 9. glove = love; 10. narrow = arrow;
11. twin = win; 12. plane = lane; 13. scent = cent; 14. smile = mile;
15. snail = nail; 16. switch = witch; 17. female = e-mail; 18. map = app;
19. notion = ocean; 20. show = hoe

Don't Think Twice: The Nickname Edition (page 99)
1. Margaret; 2. James; 3. Charles; 4. Richard; 5. Margaret; 6. Robert;
7. William; 8. Elizabeth; 9. John; 10. Alexander; 11. Christopher

Two Truths and a Lie: History Edition (page 100)
1. C: The White House wasn't completed until after Washington was president. The first president to occupy the White House was John Adams (for a few months).
2. C: King Charles ruled France from 898–922. He was the son of Louis the Stammerer. Bill Clinton was known as Slick Willie because he always seemed to be able to get out of trouble.
3. B: Sorry, no vampires for Lincoln, although both Jimmy Carter and Ronald Reagan admitted to seeing UFOs, and Teddy Roosevelt recounted a Bigfoot encounter in his book *The Wilderness Hunter*.
4. B: Queen Elizabeth does not steal spoons. At least, not that we know of.
5. A: Michael Jackson visited the White House when he was alive, but not after he died.
6. A: There was no Lord Bathespane.
7. C: There is no evidence of any presidents keeping giant snakes as pets, although Teddy Roosevelt's daughter, Alice, had a pet garter snake named Emily Spinach.
8. B: Though that would have been a fun game . . . unless you were the cow.
9. C: Sure, people will do just about anything to appear royal; however, a burning tie would have been a tad too much for loyal subjects.

10. A: Until the early 1900s, just about anyone could walk right into the White House and check the place out. Presidents and their families had a difficult time getting any privacy.

Classic Riddles & Conundrums (page 104)

1. A river; 2. His breath; 3. An egg; 4. Charcoal; 5. A person: He crawls as a baby, walks upright as an adult, and walks with a cane when he's old; 6. Parents; 7. "Are you asleep?"; 8. A candle; 9. An umbrella; 10. Silence; 11. A person riding a horse; 12. A dictionary; 13. An eye; 14. Tomorrow; 15. A coffin; 16. An ear of corn or a chicken; 17. A hole; 18. A tissue; 19. Your name; 20. A towel; Bonus: The word *stable*. Behead it and it's *table*; behead it again and it's *able*!

Word Jumbles (page 110)

1. eye, jelly, boxcar: JOY; 2. away, entitled, skateboard: TWISTER; 3. send, crypt, pencil, assistant: PARADISE; 4. chess, writer, aardvark, drought, helium: HEADACHES; 5. digest, spirit, ransom, lettuce: COMPUTER

How Many . . . (page 112)

11 rectangles and squares; 35 triangles; 23 rectangles and squares

OH, LOOK! AN EMPTY PAGE! WHAT CAN YOU DO WITH IT?